THAT'S ALL FOLKS!

The cinemas of Hastings & St. Leonards

By Nick Prince

Published in 1996 by the
MERCIA CINEMA SOCIETY
19 Pinder's Grove
Wakefield, WF1 4AH
Telephone: (01924) 372748

Typeset and Printed by FM Repro Ltd.
69 Lumb Lane, Roberttown, Liversedge, West Yorks. WF15 7NB
Telephone: (01924) 411011

Front cover: *The Public Hall Cinema (later the Orion)*
Back cover: *The Regal*

For Ron Stewart, who retired as manager of the Cannon, Hastings, in July 1995 after enjoying a 50-year career in the cinema industry.

Ron Stewart

Many thanks to the following, without whose help with information or photographs, this book would not have been possible:

Hastings Reference Library, and in particular Brion Purdey, Brian Scott, Paddy Padgem and Pamela Haines, 1066 Newspapers for allowing me to use photographs and quotes from the Hastings & St. Leonards Observer, Hastings Pictorial Advertiser, Hastings News, Hastings Herald, Hastings (Channel 5) Champion, Hastings People (later Weekend People), Nick Hobdell, Russell Claughton, BBC Radio Sussex, Evening Argus, Sussex Express & County Herald, Leslie Adams, Ted Adams, Ted Bottle, Fred Bull, Cannon Screen Entertainment, Edna Cross (Shelmordine), Bryan Denning, Barry Funnell, Hastings Talking Newspaper for the blind, David Jones, Vicky Kay, Jack and Sonia London, Alan McCann, John Manwaring Baines, Albert Morris, the late Eric Rhodes, Screen International, the late Frank Searcy, Oliver Sproxton, Ron Stewart, the late Charles Tester, the late Harry Veness, Peter Wareham.

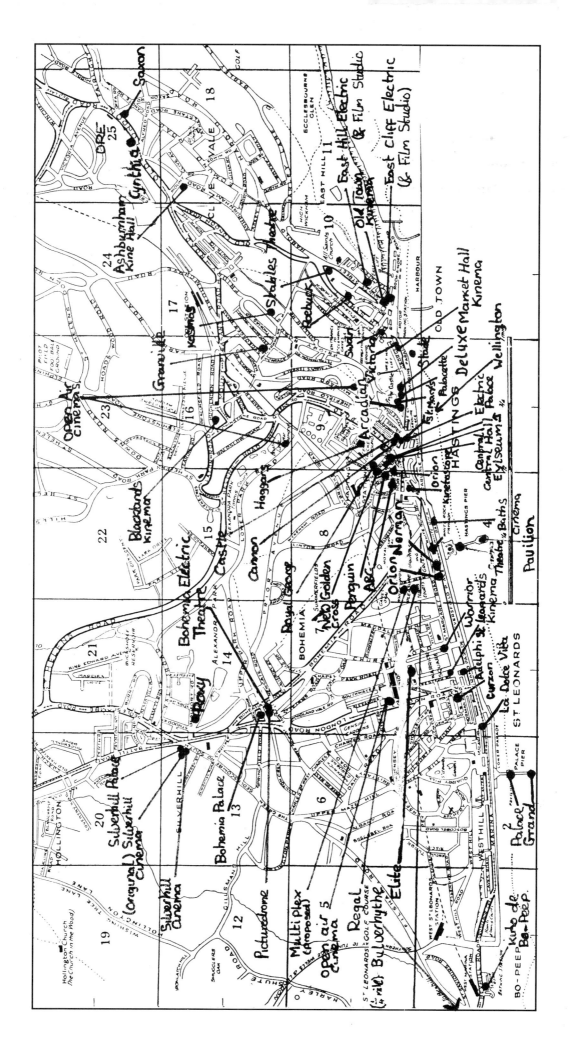

v

Introduction

Oxford had one cinema seat per 15 inhabitants, Reading and Worthing one for every 11, Brighton & Hove one for every seven, and then there was Hastings & St. Leonards which boasted the highest national average by having one cinema seat for every 3.2 inhabitants. Right from the early days Hastings had been at the forefront of the cinema revolution. As early as 1890 locals were paying to see magic lantern shows. In 1895 it was the Kinetoscope and a year later the first projected motion pictures were presented on St. Leonards' pier. By 1902 the town had its own permanent cinemas. Within a decade everyone seemed to be trying to open cinemas in the Borough as pubs converted their function rooms into cinemas. Slaughter houses, swimming baths, public halls, arcades, shops and houses all presented films to the public; some of these lasted only two or three months.

Every film outlet in the Borough is listed in this book, from the magnificent ABC Ritz and ABC Regal through to fleapits in Bohemia.

Most will remember the Ritz, De Luxe, Orion, Curzon, Regal and Roxy. Some will recall the Elite, and a few will remember the Cynthia (Ore), Central and Palacette, but just how many can remember seeing films at the Kosmos, Elyseum, Baths Cinema, Electric Palace, Victoria, Ashburnham Kine Hall, Bulverhythe, or the Kino de Bo Peep?

It seems ironic that the town that presented the UK's first Saturday matinee for children (1912), had the UK's largest cinema (1910), and came very close to opening the first purpose-built cinema (1907), should also be the town that would later claim to be the home of television.

That's All Folks is the outcome of over a decade's research into local cinema. Enjoy the memories . . .

Nick Prince

Nick Prince is co-author of Mercia Cinema Society's booklet, *Researching the History of Cinemas.*

(1) ABC Cinema

Cambridge Road, Town Centre, Hastings

Ritz Cinema — ABC Ritz — ABC Cinema

CINEMA: 1938 - 71

UNION CINEMAS LTD, who already controlled three other Hastings & St. Leonards cinemas, started work on constructing the Ritz Cinema on a site in Cambridge Road during 1937.

Just prior to completion, the Union circuit went bankrupt and all but six of their cinemas passed directly over to ABC (Associated British Cinemas).

Nine months and £110,000 later the Ritz was ready to welcome a capacity audience of 1,984. At the Grand Gala Ceremony on Saturday, 19th March 1938, Alderman E. Ford (Mayor) congratulated ABC Ltd. on 'An entertainment hall of such magnificence and enterprise.' The 'invited' audience then saw the British Premiere of the Greta Garbo film, *Marie Waleswska.*

Patrons could take advantage of the Ritz café, where one could choose from a wide range of morning coffee, light and full lunches and afternoon or full cream teas, whilst the auditorium was equipped with the latest fixtures and fittings. The Ritz's features were graced by a Wurlitzer organ.

The ABC Minors started one Saturday morning in 1946 and continued throughout the following 25 years.

After the war the cinema was known officially as the ABC Ritz but lost its identity less than 15 years later when it was simply called the ABC Cinema.

The 'mighty' Wurlitzer was removed during 1964, when the cinema was completely modernised — it was at this time that the ABC became one of the town's main live venues too, when stars such as Cliff Richard, The Shadows, Billy Fury and Mark Wynter appeared on stage.

Between 1969 and 1971, rumours became rife that the ABC was under threat; this was even more apparent to people within the industry when ABC cancelled a franchise agreement with Wimpy International, in which the old café was to become a Wimpy restaurant.

Then everyone's worst fears were confirmed, when a letter arrived informing staff that the Hastings ABC was to shut in a month's time.

Sainsbury's had bought the super cinema and had plans passed in which they could demolish the ABC and build a large supermarket.

Closure came after a screening of *Le Mans* on Wednesday, 6th October 1971. Demolition commenced during December, during which the site was excavated because an old Augustine Priory was unearthed when the foundations were laid back in 1937.

Sainsbury's opened their new supermarket in August 1974, which would later become a Co-op, who have since closed the store and left the building derelict.

Closure was extremely sad, not only in a sentimental way but because during its final summer the ABC had broken its house record twice.

Many had made life-long careers at the ABC Ritz. Among these were Eric Dunk (Chief Operator), who had worked for the company since 1935 and been at Hastings for 17 years, Miss Lily Breeds had cleaned there since the outbreak of war, whilst her fellow cleaners, Mrs. Rose Makinson and Mrs. Ethel Hodge had been sweeping the aisles since 1947 and 1951 respectively.

ABC 1 - 3 — *see Cannon*
ABC Regal — *see Regal Theatre*
ABC Ritz — *see ABC Cinema*

Exterior of Ritz, Hastings in 1946.

Exterior of ABC Ritz, Cambridge Road
— dressed up for the Coronation in June 1953.

The Ritz Cinema, Cambridge Road, Hastings, with its 'mighty' Wurlitzer.

Long Service
By the Sea

From *ABC News* dated July 1965.

Left : District Manager P. F. Jewett presents a 15 years' Long Service Badge and Cheque to Miss J. RICHARDS, at the ABC, Hastings. Looking on are Manager S. H. Winterson (centre) and members of the staff.

August 1961.

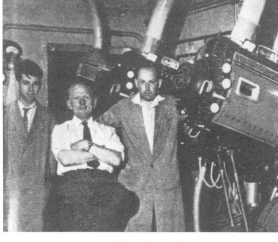

RITZ, HASTINGS

W. Milne (Proationer), E. Dunk (Chief) and R. Randall (2nd). A 4th member of the team (P. Burton, 3rd) was on holiday when the picture was taken.

January 1963.

Left : Mrs. L. MAKINSON, Cleaner at the ABC, Hastings (Manager E. L. Shelmerdine at the time), is rewarded for 15 years' devotion to duty by District Manager L. H. T. Hodson.

September 1966.

900th Anniversary at HASTINGS

ABC 1966 contributed to the AD 1066 celebrations with a Road safety Quiz. We picture right the Mayor of Hastings (Cllr. D. W. Wilshin) presenting awards at the ABC, Hastings. Manager **B. F. Denning** is central, with Hastings Road Safety Organiser Mr. George Sheppard right. It was a knock-out contest running for ten weeks, arousing great interest in the town, and enlightening scores of young people as to the rules of the Highway Code. The Mayor afterwards told the Press : " This competition, instituted by our Road Safety Organiser and the Manager of the ABC Cinema, has tied up very well with our 900th Anniversary Celebration Year and I congratulate them on behalf of the town." The campaign gained nineteen separate press reports.

Various cuttings from *ABC News,* concerning various issues at the ABC (Ritz).

Interior of the ABC, Cambridge Road, Hastings — shortly before closure.

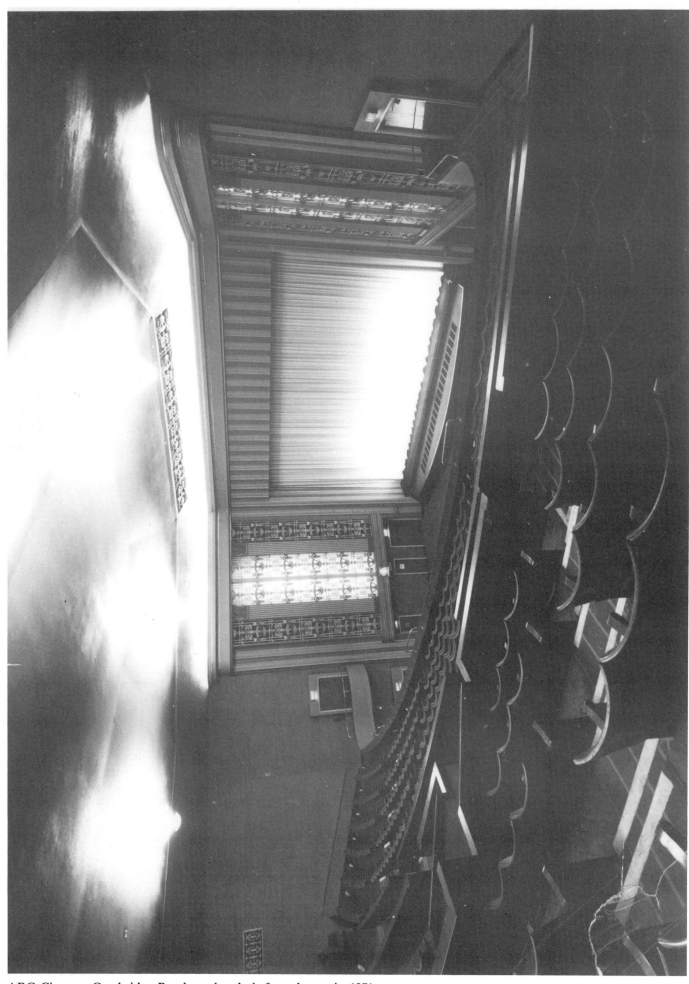

ABC Cinema, Cambridge Road — shortly before closure in 1971.

A fire burns in the auditorium of the ABC in December 1971 — it was started by workmen who were burning some old fixtures.

The final advert for the ABC in 1971.

The cleared ABC site (1972) ready to welcome archaeologists and later a Sainsbury's supermarket.

(2) Adelphi Kinetoscope
Adelphi Hotel, Warrior Square, Central St. Leonards-on-sea

Adelphi Kinetoscope — Adelphi Bioscope

CINEMA: 1895 and 1902

Between July and September 1895, the Edison Kinetoscope was enjoying its St. Leonards' debut. The Kinetoscope is basically a set-up that is similar to a 'What the Butler Saw' peep show, the only difference being that the Kinetoscope used filmstock instead of photographs — an average film would last for three minutes.

Films returned to this venue for a Bioscope (primitive cinema) season during 1902. No other public screenings have been given since.

---

(3) Arcadian
Pelham Arcade, Pelham Place, Old Town, Hastings

CINEMA: 1907 - 1911

The Pelham Arcadian was one of two cinemas to operate in the Pelham Arcade. It was part of the Pelham Hall Assembly Rooms complex and screened its first motion picture in 1907. Films were presented at erratic intervals and the Arcadian hardly ever advertised. It screened its final movie in 1911 when the tiny hall was engulfed by the auditorium of the Palacette Cinema.

See also Pelham Palacette.

---

(4) Ashburnham Kine-Hall
Junction Ashburnham Road and Mount Road, Clive Vale, Hastings

Clive Vale Assembly Rooms — Ashburnham Kine-Hall — Clive Vale Kine-Hall — St. Mary's Social Club

CINEMA: 1912 - 1913

The Clive Vale Assembly Rooms were built in 1890, when the building was used for every conceivable form of entertainment. Bioscope shows made rare visits from 1902 and a decade later all other types of entertainment were dropped in favour of films.

Between July and November 1912, it was called the Ashburnham Kine-Hall; other forms of entertainment took place until July 1913 when it re-opened as the Clive Vale Kine-Hall. The final closure occurred three months later. It continued as an Assembly Room for some years and the premises are now occupied by the St. Mary's Social Club.

---

(5) Baths Cinema
(Private Baths), White Rock Baths, White Rock, Hastings

CINEMA: 1913 - 1915

During the dying days of 1912, the Private Baths at the White Rock Swimming Baths were leased by Colonel Newitt, who immediately set about transforming it into a cinema with seating for 1,616.

The aptly titled Baths Cinema opened on Saturday, 20th February 1913, with the British premiere of *Duty Stronger than Love* which became the first of many such premieres to be presented at this peculiar venue.

Films made way for concerts during the winter months of 1913/14 and 1914/15. The Baths Cinema closed down in March 1915, after its lease expired. It reverted back to a swimming bath, which was

Baths Cinema, White Rock, Hastings, in 1913.

acquired by the corporation in later years. More recently the old cinema has been a skateboarding park, an Ice Skating Rink and Roller Disco. It is currently still under the control of Hastings Ice Rink, which now has a larger rink next door. The Baths Cinema is believed to have been the UK's first picture palace to have had an underground auditorium.

---

(6) Blacklands Kinema
Blacklands Community Centre, Hughenden Road, Blacklands, Hastings

CINEMA: 1911 (Only)

Another local cinema that was very short-lived was the Blacklands Kinema, which operated during the high season of 1911 only for three days a week. It is now the Blacklands Community Centre.

---

(7) Bohemia Electric Theatre
Bohemia Road, Bohemia, St. Leonards-on-sea

Bohemia Electric Theatre — Bohemia Picture Theatre

CINEMA: 1912 (Only)

ADVERTISING SLOGAN: *The Red Front Picture-Hall.*

Europe's smallest public cinema opened at 3 pm on Saturday, 27th January 1912. The auditorium of the Bohemia Electric Theatre was a converted first-floor bedroom, where 25 patrons could huddle together on a handful of benches in the freezing winter temperature — should they have the desire.

The old Bohemia Electric Theatre.

Films were screened through a hole in the ceiling from a hand-cranked projector in the loft. According to one elderly Hastings resident the screen was a sheet tacked on to a board, which was rested on the seats of a couple of chairs at an angle, in order to pick up the projector beam.

Newsreels were supplied by Gaumont Graphic and refreshments were given away free of charge during matinées.

The Bohemia Electric Theatre's claim to fame is the fact that it is the earliest known cinema to present a Saturday children's matinée, the first of which was given on Saturday, 3rd February 1912.

The average performance lasted for a mere half-an-hour. This is because that was the only possible way that it could make any type of profit due to its tiny capacity.

After a few months the cinema was shut and its owners, the pompously titled Imperial Cinematograph Company were broke.

However all was not lost though, when the flea pit was taken over by a Mr. Preston, who immediately set about making improvements. These included an extended capacity of fifty and such new-fangled facilities as seating and lavatories. It opened as the Bohemia Picture Theatre on 1st June 1912 and advertised itself as the Redfront Picture Hall. Free oranges were given out at each performance.

Preston too was unsuccessful and the cinema shut during December 1912. It became a shop and now forms the left-hand side of Lullabuy's pram shop at 70 Bohemia Road. A sky-light that was once used by the projectionist all those years ago is still visible from the road.

---

(8) Bohemia Palace
Lower South Road, Bohemia, St. Leonards-on-sea

CINEMA: 1912 (Only)

This tiny cinema screened films between August and December 1912. It had room for around 80 patrons. It is now occupied by Scott James Glass and was situated on the left-hand side of the Bohemia Road junction.

---

(9) Bohemia Picturedrome

Lower South Road, Bohemia, St. Leonards-on-sea

CINEMA: 1912 - 1913

Opposite the Bohemia Palace was another short-lived cinema, which is also currently situated by Scott James Glass. Don't be fooled by the prestigious building which looked like it was a purpose-built cinema. The truth is that only a tiny part of it, possibly on the first floor, was used for films. It opened in October 1912 but was shut by April 1913.

Bohemia Picture Theatre — *see Bohemia Electric Theatre*
Bo Peep — *see Kino de Bo Peep*

---

(10) Bulverhythe Kinema

Bulverhythe Road, Bulverhythe, St. Leonards-on-sea

During the research of this book I met only a mere two people who can remember going to this cinema as youngsters. Apparently it was situated at the rear of the old Gable's Stores opposite the Bulverhythe Public House. It operated from 1912 until 1913.

---

(11) Cannon Cinemas

Queens Road, Town Centre, Hastings

**Gaiety Theatre — Gaiety Picture Theatre — Gaiety Cinema — Classic Cinema —
Classic (1 & 2) Cinemas — Cannon Classic — Cannon Cinemas — ABC 1 - 3**

CINEMA: 1932 (Open)

It will be during March 1997 that Hastings' sole surviving cinema will take over as the venue that has spent the longest time screening films to the borough — the record is currently held by the Orion.

We must go back 114 years, to 1882 to trace its history when as the Gaiety theatre it came to life on 1st August. During those early days it enjoyed an interesting life and among the famous and infamous to have trodden its boards are Harry Houdini and Winchelsea resident Lily Langtry. William Gladstone once spoke there for an hour and a half and was almost killed on the way to the Gaiety.

The theatre's Director was local personality George Gaze (d1913) who was mentioned in a July edition of *The Stage* during 1888. The article read; 'Mr. Gaze . . . has been experimenting very successfully with the telephone on the stage. He has three transmitters placed there, one in each wing and one in the centre close to the floodlights. The speaking, singing and music were heard very distinctly in different parts of the town.'

The 1,400 seater was refurbished in 1888 and again in 1898 and four years later occasional film shows were presented, although it would be another thirty years until it would become a full-time cinema.

During the first week of May 1932, the Gaiety presented the Hastleon's production of *The Desert Song* which proved so successful that it was retained for a second week and ended its run on Saturday, 14th May. There were to be no more shows and the three-tier theatre along with its eight private boxes was gutted and turned into a two-tier 1,100 seat cinema.

Kinema Playhouse Ltd, who operated many local cinemas, were the new owners and it was under the presence of Director Randolph E. Richards, that it opened on Monday, 12th December 1932 with *Rome Express*. The support programme that day included the Laurel and Hardy Oscar winning short, *The Music Box*.

Souvenir.

GAIETY THEATRE, HASTINGS.

Fifty Years of ———
Music, Comedy and Drama.

Opened
August 1st, 1882.

Closed
May 21st, 1932.

Crowds forming outside the Gaiety Theatre, Queens Road (circa 1912).

Oil painting of the Gaiety Theatre (date unknown). Note the Gaiety Restaurant (later Gaiety pub) situated where the present cinema entrance is.

Interior of the four-tier Gaiety Theatre (date unknown).

The Theatre bids you Farewell — The Gaiety theatre closes after 50 years of live shows.

The opening advert for the
Gaiety Theatre (December 1932).

In its 64 years as a cinema, the Gaiety (Cannon) has enjoyed many first runs. Throughout the 1950s, 60s and part of the 70s it was a pre-release cinema.

15

Classic 2 comes to life in May 1971.

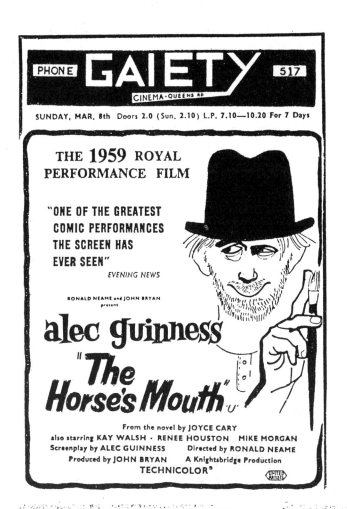

Exterior views of the Classic 1 and 2.

Actor Malcolm McDowell cuts the 'new' Classic 2 cake. Manager Leslie Cragg (left) looks on.

Preparing for the new triple-screen Classic.

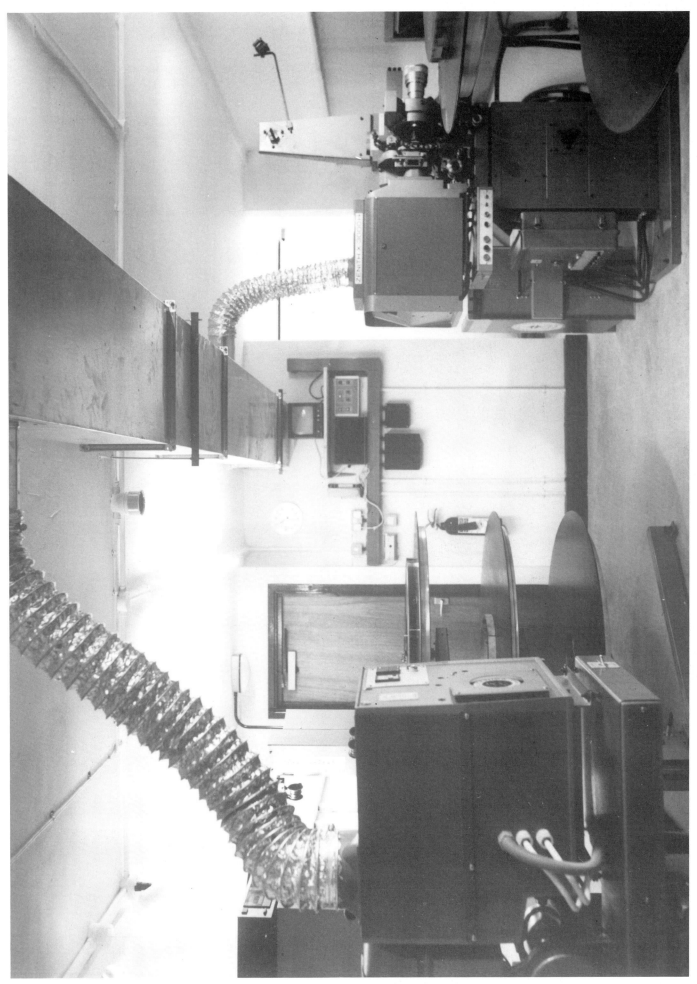

Operating box to Cannon 2 (right) and Cannon 3 (left) — 1985.

Right: Cannon 1 (1985).
Below: Cannon 2 (1985).
Bottom right: Cannon 3 (1985).

Screen One.

Screen Three.

Screen Two.

20

Capital & Provincial Theatres (Classic) took over in 1966 and the following year the Gaiety Cinema got a Classic transformation when it was renamed Classic.

On Friday, 27th May 1971, the Classic became the first Sussex cinema to be twinned; the circle and front stalls became the 767-seat Classic One, whilst the rear stalls were sectioned off to form a 165-seat Classic Two. The first film in Screen Two was *Raging Bull* starring Malcolm McDowell, who also publicly opened the cinema.

In·the early 1980s Classic sold out to Cannon and in 1984 work started on rebuilding the interior as a triple cinema complex.

The three-screen luxury cinema came with arm-chair French-style seating (with each costing over £100), state of the art projection equipment, dolby stereo in the largest cinema, a Wimpy Bar and licensed bar.

The proposed Wimpy ended up being a drug store and the licensed bar never materialised either. During my time at the cinema, I found quite adequate facilities by sneaking out of the side exit and slipping into the nearby Clown in Russell Street.

The Cannon Classic opened on Friday, 21st June 1985, with a gala charity opening. The 393-seat Screen One opened with *A View to a Kill;* the 178-seat Screen Two came to life with *A Passage to India;* and the 129-seat Screen Three opened with *Grace Quigley.* All three films officially opened to the public the following day. In December 1985 the cinema was renamed Classic Cinemas.

Between 1985 and 1995, the Cannon's Manager was Ron Stewart, who retired in July '95 after 50 years in the business.

The Cannon continues to be successful and during the school holidays queues can often be seen winding up Albert Road. It has been the Borough's sole surviving 'Public' cinema since the Orion closed in 1978. In December 1985 the cinema was re-named Cannon Cinemas and on Friday 7th June, 1996 became the ABC.

Cannon Classic — *see Cannon Cinemas*

---

(12) Castle Bioscope
Castle Hotel, Wellington Square / Albert Road, Town Centre, Hastings

CINEMA: Early 1900s

Occasional bioscope shows were presented at the Castle Hotel between circa 1905 and 1907. The Hotel was demolished in 1966 to make way for the old town centre Tesco store, which in turn has become Hastings Indoor Market and the Victoria Snooker Centre.

Castle Hotel Kinema — *see Castle Bioscope*
Castle Kinema — *see Castle Bioscope*

---

(13) Central Hall Cinema
Lower Central Hall, Bank Buildings, Station Road, Town Centre, Hastings

CINEMA: 1911 (Only)

Between April and October 1911 films were screened three days a week at the Lower Central Hall, which at the time was leased to the Police for use as a Social Club. The short-lived venture rarely advertised and was called the Central Hall Cinema. It was in no way associated with the Central Picture Theatre, which was situated in the Upper Central Hall.

---

(14) Central Picture Theatre
Upper Central Hall, Bank Buildings, Station Road, Town Centre, Hastings

CINEMA: 1910 - 25

ADVERTISING SLOGANS: *The one with the red light outside.*
The one with the ruby light outside.
The house of no vulgarity.

NICKNAMES: *The red light.*
The whore-house.

During the Autumn of 1910, the local catering firm Atkins Bros. & Cox, took over the lease of the Upper Central Hall and converted it into a 260-seat venue, which came to life on Tuesday, 1st November with *The Telephone* which was reported as being a powerful documentary of a fire and showed how one would call the fire brigade by means of the telephone.

The Central Picture Theatre opened for business every day except for Sunday — it even showed films on Christmas Day. Tea and biscuits were served at all performances but were supplied free of charge between 4.30 pm and 5.30 pm.

Special promotion films were frequently booked in conjunction with local institutions. During its first year of business the Central presented mainly short films which each lasted for around ten minutes. These made way for feature films in October 1911 — a move that upset opposition cinemas, many of which made serious accusations about the Central.

One such accusation led to the following advert placed in the Hastings and St. Leonards Observer during early 1912. It read: *'I beg to announce that I will give £5 to any local institution named by anyone who can prove that the film advertised and shown at my screen as long ago as the 23rd October last of the recent eruption of Mount Etna was not a genuine photograph, can rely that it is so.*

Yours Faithfully
Whyte Jones.'

Albert Morris, now in his 99th year, was employed as an 'Odd-bod' at the Central Picture Theatre between 1913 and 1915. Mr. Morris had to do a bit of everything which included helping in the projection box, sweeping, sticking up posters on his morning off and working on the sound effects — the wages in those days were 6s. for a six and a half day week.

The Central never had its name up outside nor did it have any front doors but there was an old iron gate that was locked up at night.

Some antiquated wooden steps led up to the pay box, behind which were two doors that had tiny windows fitted so that the cashier would know when there was an intermission or change of house.

The operating box was a small concrete room, which was built on a wooden platform and the screen stood in front of two scaffolding towers.

The Central seems to have been somewhat elaborate compared to some of the antiquated dumps that attempted to show films in the Borough.

Ornate gas jet lamps covered with orangey red shades brightened up the side walls during intervals and were placed about half-way up the wall. Below these was dark oak panelling and above the lamps was some deep red wallpaper which went up to ceiling level.

6d. would get you into the best seats, which were well-cushioned and fitted on a raked floor, while the cheaper seats were placed on the flat floor at the front of the hall and were merely covered with leatherette. The aisles and front were covered with coconut matting carpet.

Seven people were employed at the Central. These were the Manager, Odd-bod, Sound Effects expert, Projectionist, Assistant Projectionist, two part-time Pianists and the Cashier.

In those days the most important person in the cinema was the Sound Effects expert, who merrily sat on a hard wooden chair by the screen nine hours a day clacking coconuts for scenes that had horses in, rolling drums during war scenes and ringing bells and blowing whistles during chase scenes.

Situated opposite the Sound Effects expert was an upright piano which was tinkled at all times, even during newsreels. Mrs. Lawes was the afternoon pianist, whilst Mrs. Collins played in the evenings. Her son Andrew later became a famous composer. At 10.30 p.m. (sharp) the final film ended and the piano stopped tinkling as Mrs. Collins could be seen making a dash across the Memorial in the hope of catching the last tram to her West Hill home. As the last tram was due to leave at 10.30 p.m. she more often than not missed the 'damned thing'.

Customers were kept up to date with world issues by the Pathé Gazette, which was made by Topical Budget Pictures. Mr. Morris remembers that the Central shared the same copy as the nearby Royal Cinema De Luxe and he recalled, 'After they had screened it, their Odd-bod would return it to us; this procedure could be done up to four times a day.'

During February 1915 the then proprietors, Whyte Jones and a Mr. Petty, were no longer seeing eye to eye and before their partnership was terminated they ended up bickering in the High Court.

Soon after the Great War had ended, Harry Furniss, who had premiered many of his films at the Central, took over its lease and ran it into the 1920s.

Soon after Furniss's death in 1925, the Central Picture Theatre's screen flickered for the very last time. The premises had been ordered to close by the local Fire Brigade on the grounds that there weren't enough exits. This coupled with the old wooden steps from the pavement, which still exist 71 years after closure, made the poor old Central a 'death trap'.

The final Cinema to close in Hastings, that never installed sound, closed after a screening of
A Pictorial Tour through Canada on 30th March 1925. The stars of the silent era such as John Bunny, Fatty Arbuckle, Little Tich et un Big Boots, Charlie Chaplin Super Clown, Mabel Normand (the Bathing Beauty) and Pearl White (every lad's dream girl), were no more.

During World War II, the Central Hall was used to give out gas-masks and towards the end of the War it became a public shelter for local residents who had become homeless during the blitz and in 1946 it enjoyed a short life as the Central Children's Theatre, which opened with *Ali Baba*.

More recently it has been used by Elim Church and is currently a recreation and advice centre for the homeless, unemployed and those in need of help. Attempts to re-open it as a cinema and to turn it into a Synagogue both failed during the 1980s.

Cinema de Loo — *see De Luxe Cinema*
Cinema De Luxe — *see De Luxe Cinema*
Cinthia — *see Cynthia*
Classic — *see Cannon Cinemas*
Clive Vale Cinema — *see Cynthia*
Clive Vale Kine-Hall — *see Ashburnham Kine-Hall*
Continental — *see Roxy*
Continentale — *see Roxy*
Cosmos — *see Kosmos Kinema*

----

(15) Curzon Cinema
Norman Road and Shepherd Street (pre- 1922), Central St. Leonards-on-sea

Kinema Palace — The Kinema — Curzon Cinema — Curzon Cinema and Vogue Social Club — Curzon Cinema

CINEMA: 1913 - 1977

The Kinema Palace became the first purpose-built cinema to open in St. Leonards — albeit by a mere 22 days.

The 650-seater opened on Wednesday, 5th November 1913, and at the time was described as 'ultra-advanced'. The auditorium departed from the usual tunnel style and was square, with its ceiling covered by fancy plaster shapes. In addition to this the cinema could also boast the best ventilation in the United Kingdom.

The walls of the auditorium were covered with teak panelling, whilst its screen was the first in St. Leonards-on-sea to be covered by automatic electric curtains during intervals — these incidentally were violet and green.

The Kinema Playhouse was controlled for the majority of its cinematic life by Kinema Playhouse Ltd. It was re-named the Kinema during the first week of July 1921.

During the Second World War there were two attempts on the Kinema's life. The first of these occurred on Sunday, 23rd May 1943, when a large German bomb that was aimed at the picture house missed its target but flattened half of the Warrior Gate pub killing 25. The second attempt to end its reign was shortly afterwards when other bombs missed the Kinema but destroyed many premises half-way up Norman Road.

Back in the days of the Great War, whilst the Kinema Palace was in its infancy, the newsreel screened at each performance was the Kinema Palace News — a local Newsreel that encouraged a regular local patronage who came in to see each edition of the reel in case they had been caught on it. Another popular aspect from those early days was that the cinema didn't issue tickets. Instead patrons were given a metal disk.

In 1952 the Kinema was totally modernised and during the spring of that year the old Edwardian frontage was replaced by the modern 1950s style facade that most will remember.

During this refit, larger new seats were installed which reduced its capacity to 476. It was at this time that the Shepherd Street entrance became used as an exit only.

Kinema Playhouse Ltd. sold the Curzon to Capital and Provincial Cinemas Ltd. (Classic) in 1966 and a later the Curzon was under threat from bingo.

Permission was refused to turn the cinema to bingo and for the following four years there were many attempts by Classic to turn it into a leisure centre, social club, sex cinema and so on. The closest it ever got to changing use was in 1971 when the proprietors got as far as having perspex signs made for the Vogue Cinema and Social Club — these however, were never installed. A year later bingo was due to arrive five nights per week with films on the other two — this also failed to materialise.

Classic passed the building's lease on to Andego Enterprises Ltd. in 1974 and it was from this point that the Classic in Hastings had a 4/5ths bar on the Curzon. In other words the Norman Road cinema could only have one release in five on the first run.

During the next two years the Curzon lost a great deal of money but during 1976 the losses had been reduced to around £200 per week.

The end came very suddenly and shocked the Borough. On Monday, 18th January 1977, the Manager, Mr. Frank Searcy told the Hastings News; 'I asked Mr. Rhodes (Proprietor) about a missing programme and he said there would be no need to worry about it as the cinema would have to close on Saturday'.

Raid on Entebbe was the film to be screened and after the evening performance on Saturday, 23rd

As the Kinema (1930s).

A bomb intended for the Kinema, missed its target and hit the Warrior Gate pub instead, destroying half of it — St. Leonards Post Office now stands on the site (1943).

This photo of the 1950s facade was taken on Monday 18th January 1977 — the day that its closure was announced. Six days later, the Curzon, St. Leonards' last cinema, was no more.

SHOCK CLOSURE OF LOSS MAKING CURZON CINEMA

by Tom Maitland

FRANK SEARCY

RELIEF manager Miss Vera Deeprose.

How the *Hastings News* announced the closure of St. Leonards' last cinema (1977). Mr. Searcy (pictured) had worked there since 1928.

Charles Bronson leads
the final roll of credits in 1977.

27

January 1977 the Curzon ended its 64-year film career as the cinema industry took its final curtain call in St. Leonards.

Searcy had started at the cinema back in 1928; his wife had been secretary for 15 years, his son and daughter both worked there at weekends; Very Deeprose (Assistant Manager) and Alice Jordan (Cashier) had been there for 11 years and David Sarkies (Projectionist) nine years.

Closure occurred a week after the Penguin Cinema's demise in the Town Centre and less than two weeks later the White Rock Theatre would show its last film.

Mr. Searcy retired and died in May 1995 and his wife passed away a year earlier. Almost everyone who went to the cinema during the last 25 or so years will recall Mr. Searcy's squeaky tea trolley that was wheeled out at each interval.

In the late 1980s the Norman Road entrance was demolished although the old Shepherd Street entrance survives. The proscenium and exit door are still visible — the latter still reads 'Curzon Cinema — Exit Only.' It is now occupied by Brooker's Builders Merchants.

---

(16) Cynthia Cinema
Old London Road, Ore Village, Hastings

Cynthia Cinema — Ore Cinema — Clive Vale Cinema — Princess

CINEMA: 1913 - 1923

ADVERTISING SLOGAN: *The Cheapest, Cosiest and the Best!*

NICKNAMES: *The Cosy.*
The Cyn.
Woody's.

A six week building programme commenced in mid-December 1906 on a site situated on the border of Ore and Clive Vale. Had the work been completed the cinema would have been the very first purpose-built picture palace to have opened in the United Kingdom but sadly the contractors went bankrupt in the process.

The building remained half-completed for the next six years until work re-started, which resulted in the Cynthia Cinema opening on Tuesday, 3rd June 1913.

Within weeks it had become THE place in town and less than a year later the ten minute shorts were replaced by feature films, the first of which was *The Boy Scout Hero* which was on its first run in Hastings. Over the next couple of months many other first runs were enjoyed by the Cynthia. Its opposition cinemas in Hastings were far from happy about this situation and succeeded in having the Ore cinema barred from having further first runs.

Between 1914 and 1919 the proprietor was Rod B. Bowden who ran it as the Ore Cinema but on Monday, 19th May 1919 the Comedian Jimmy Woods took over the lease — Woods put on cine-variety. This was the first time that stage had been presented in Ore since the Hare and Hounds Theatre burned down 96 years earlier. It was during Woods' ownership that it was named the Clive Vale Cinema.

Mr. T. Morgan took over on 19th May 1921 and renamed it the Princess Cinema and exactly a year later Alfred Robotham took over. Despite making a profit, the ten-year lease wasn't renewed and the Princess closed on Saturday, 19th May 1923. The closure was apparently due to a three-fold rent increase. It became a furniture store and is now used as a Salvation Army hall.

De Loo — *see De Luxe Cinema*

The new Cynthia Cinema, Ore village (1913).

As the Ore Cinema (1914).

29

(17) De Luxe Cinema
Pelham Place, Old Town, Hastings

Empire Theatre of Varieties — Marine Theatre of Varieties — The Hippodrome —
Royal Cinema Deluxe — Cinema De Luxe — Union Cinema de Luxe — Deluxe Cinema —
Cinema Deluxe Bingo — De Luxe Bingo — De Luxe Leisure Centre

CINEMA: 1910 - 1965 (1970)

NICKNAMES: *De Loo.*
          Gooin' Furrin.

A whole century has now passed since the old Marine Hotel and bars were demolished to make way for a Victoria Music-Hall on Hastings Sea Front.

Only the facade of the magnificent building that replaced the Hotel exists into the present day. This fine example of what a traditional music hall was like is now a snooker club, bingo club, amusement arcade, bar and so on . . .

It came to life as the Empire Theatre of Varieties on Easter Saturday 1899 — for those of you that aren't old enough to remember Easter 1899 it fell on 2nd April, with All Fools day being the 1st.

It was designed by infamous architects Ernest Runtz & Co. of London, who apparently, for one reason or another, which remains a mystery to theatre historians, gave their services free.

The auditorium covered a superficial area of some 7,860 feet and had a facade of 131 feet. By all accounts the 'Champagne was flowing more liberally than the sea outside' on that night.

One can't but notice the two large copper domes that grace its roof even to this day — these can be greatly appreciated by looking on from the West Hill or the castle — thankfully they have survived numerous attempts and threats of being melted down and turned into ammunition to help the war effort.

Even to this day the building must be looked upon as the very finest piece of neo-baroque architecture to still survive mainly because it is complemented by numerous arched windows, coats of arms and a couple of balconies.

Inside though it is a most ironic story, for the entire interior was gutted (ripped to shreds) in 1970. When I tell you some of its features you will begin to appreciate what a marvellous building it really was — there isn't even a single palace of mansion in the world that has been built with such sheer splendour.

The staircases that led up to the four tiers were made of solid marble, imported to England on two ships from Italy. The hand rails were made of solid brass and plated in gold; the auditorium was graced by eight rococo private boxes. As if it wasn't enough to just have a rococo style interior in a provincial town, they were highlighted by an amazing sparkling white — the white of course was ground Ivory, which not only gilded the boxes but the circle fronts too!

Rich terra-cotta red was the colour scheme adopted throughout this beautiful building, which was glamourised with a hint of pure gold on the side walls, while the draperies were original amber satin-silk, the upholstery velvet and the floors covered by the highest possible quality neutral green Wilton Pile carpeting.

The list is endless and to be honest this building deserves a large volume all to itself.

At a preview ceremony on Thursday, 30th March 1899, Hastings' Mayor, Aldermen Tuppenny, congratulated everyone who had been responsible for the construction of the theatre — Tuppenny was especially taken aback by two particular points — the first being the 'electric light', which was the very first example he had seen and secondly by the telephone — should any of the other ten addresses in Hastings that had a 'phone installed, wish to spend an evening in this splendid theatre, all they had to do was ask the operator for Hastings 11.

A full house saw Winchelsea comedienne, Marie Lloyd, head the bill. Also appearing that evening was comedian Alec Hurley, the illusionist Carl Herts and a dance troupe called The Tillers Eight Dancers.

Admission that evening was 6d. (gallery), 1s. (second circle and pit), 2s. (stalls and grande circle), 3s. (fauteuils) and 10s. for a private box.

Two years later it was renamed the Marine Theatre of Varieties and in 1905 the Marine Palace of Varieties Company sold out to the specially formed Hippodrome Syndicate. It was the latter who suddenly closed the theatre in 1910, a move that caused the second biggest mystery and common tongue wagging during the early part of the twentieth century — incidentally the greatest cause of common chit-chat were the various sightings of the 'Hastings Sea Serpent' in 1907 (our version of the Loch Ness Monster).

The mystery didn't leave townsfolk inquisitive for too long for on 18th October 1910 the old theatre-re-opened. Only this time it was as the 2,300 seat Royal Cinema De Luxe, which at that time had the largest seating capacity of any cinema in Europe.

The opening film was *The Angel of Dawson's Claim.* A Hastings and St. Leonards' Observer reporter was present on the evening. He reported; 'An enormous crowd numbering quite a thousand awaited in the street for the doors to open, and when they did, these made a general stampede for admittance. People of all classes could be seen in the throng, some of them in evening dress having driven up in their motors, carriages, cabs or taxis'.

An equally antiquated but interesting report was given by the long defunct Hastings Pictorial Advertiser and Visitors List who penned the following tribute: 'By ten minutes to eight the house was full, but late-comers still flowed through the doors, admitted by an attendant wearing Olde English attire, after the manner of Dick Turpin. People crowded the corridors, the promenades at the rear of the circles and, in fact, squeezed themselves anywhere where they could watch the opening ceremony and subsequent picture entertainment'.

It is unofficially believed that up to a hundred local people sold items such as shoes and cookers in order to be able to get their entire families admitted for the event — apparently almost 900 more patrons were admitted than there were seats for — the total number has been reported over the years as being between 3,400 and 4,000 (around a tenth of the town's population in those days).

During the 1920s the Royal Cinema De Luxe became the Cinema Deluxe and in the 1960s the De Luxe Cinema. Over the years it has been owned by Hippodrome Ltd., Deluxe Hastings Ltd., Hastings Theatre Co. Ltd. and Union Cinemas.

Some 85+ years ago the cinema had two local nicknames, the first being De Loo is still used by locals today, but the second was forgotten more than 65 years ago. This was Gooin' Furrin — which means going foreign — or in other words the Old Towners' version of having to go to foreign parts in order to see a film — technically speaking the cinema was situated neither in the old town nor the centre, though it has an Old Town address.

Going back again briefly to those early silent days, it must be noted that in 1914 films were presented with the Edison Kinephone (film soundtrack on a record playing in sync with the film, which is exactly the same system used on the film *The Jazz Singer,* supposedly the first feature to have had sound on film — Rubbish!).

Adverts at the time read; *You see the man — you hear his voice!*
You see the dog — you hear him bark!

In later years the Cinema DeLuxe went over to the Gaumont British Circuit (later taken over by Rank) and although still breaking even — just — it was as a Rank release hall that the Ursula Andress movie *She,* became the final film to be shown at the De Luxe. This was presented on Saturday, 24th July 1965 — the support film that evening was *Jimmy Saville Presents . . . Pop Gear.*

Bingo started the following day, although the De Luxe kept its cinematograph licence just in case it wanted to revert back to film. In order to do this the De Luxe had to screen a minimum of one

The Hippodrome in 1908 (ignore the fact that it had its original name on the Canopy). Two years later it became the Royal Cinema De Luxe.

Royal Cinema De Luxe (1911).

Staff at the Cinema De Luxe (1912).

These posters were discovered
on a basement wall in 1970.

33

UP-TO-DATE ADVERTISING.

The above novel mode of advertisement has been adopted by the Management of the Royal Cinema de Luxe, where this week an excellent picture illustrating Captain Scott's Expedition to the South Pole is being shown, and which is attracting large audiences. In the background is the well-known and comfortable picture resort.

Publicity 'Street Stunt' for *Captain Scott's Expedition to the South Pole* — 1913.

Interior of the Cinema De Luxe as a bingo hall (1970).

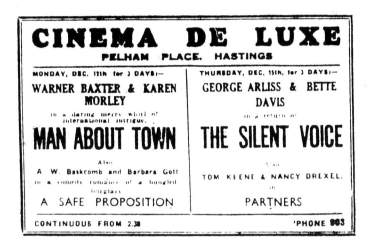

(1932).

(1959).

A drawing of East Cliff House by Thomas Hearne. Between 1902 and 1907 it was screening films under the banner East Cliff Electric Bioscope, and was a studio for Furniss Films, Hastings.

A 1930s watercolour by E. Leslie Badham showing East Hill House. In the early part of this century it was the East Hill Electric Bioscope and Film Studio.

reel (18 minutes) of film at each bingo session. This format was dropped when the ivory, gold and marble was all ripped out and floors built across at each floor level. Although the seating capacity had been reduced gradually over the years to a mere 900 due to safety reasons patrons could still use two of the four levels.

Another feature from 1899 that went into the skip along with the various minerals was a painting called The Goddess of the Sea, an original oil painting, which was ripped up and burned.

Whilst the conversion was taking place as the theatre was being turned into the De Luxe Leisure Centre, the Hastings and St. Leonards Observer of 7th March 1970 ended a report on the matter with the sub headline 'SUNSET?' and continued 'An Observer reporter writes: At a preview — 30th March, 1899 — Councillor Dr. Gray declared that as the sun never set on the British Empire he trusted that the sun on the Empire Theatre of Varieties might soon rise and never set. With the sound of builders at work this week at the De Luxe it looks as if the sun's gone down all right.' Perhaps the afore published tribute should be given not only to the Empire/De Luxe but also to the British Empire, neiher of which survived intact, though the Theatre/Cinema outlasted its namesake.

Dolce Vita — *see La Dolce Vita*
Dolphin — *see La Dolce Vita*

---

(18) East Cliff Electric Bioscope *(Cinema and Film Studio)*
Rock-A-Nore, Old Town, Hastings

CINEMA: 1902 - 07

East Cliff House was originally built for the Shakespearian commentator, censor and playwright Edward Capel.

During the early years of this century it became two separate cinemas, with the ground floor becoming the East Hill Electric Bioscope and Furniss Film Studio in 1902.

Films were presented on an average of three times a week and were all made by Harry Furniss. These film shows ended in 1907 — the 82-seater has since been used as a bingo club, Capel's Wine Bar and is now the Capel's Fish Restaurant.

---

(19) East Hill Electric Bioscope *(Cinema and Film Studio)*
Tackleway, Old Town, Hastings

CINEMA: 1902 - 1909

Harry Furniss resided at East Hill House for a great number of years. This building was the home of H.R.H. The Duke of Sussex and it is here that it is rumoured the Prince Regent kept his various ladies of 'ill repute' and regularly visited them under a variety of assumed names and disguises.

Films arrived during the first week of November 1902 and like the nearby East Cliff Electric, were all made by Furniss. There is some confusion as to when the public theatre ended but it is generally believed that from 1905 onwards only old material was screened.

Years after Furniss left East Hill House, he still rented two rooms where he kept much of his film archive — Films ended in 1909.

Electric Cinema — *See Palace Cinema*

---

(20) Electric Palace

Wellington Place, Town Centre, Hastings

CINEMA: 1910 - 15

ADVERTISING SLOGAN: *Come and see the world before your eyes!*

A disused slaughter house and food store was converted into a 200-seat cinema during late spring 1910. The premises, situated at 7a Wellington Place, opened as the Electric Palace on Monday, 4th June 1910.

The first proprietor was a Mr. Harmer but sadly, like most of the very early cinemas in town, very few details exist. It is widely believed that the cinema was highly successful, so why Harmer would wish to sell up two years later remains a mystery.

At the end of 1912 the Hastings Pictorial Advertiser and Visitors List announced that the Electric Palace had been acquired by Mr. A. H. Pollard — within weeks Pollard was running Electric Palaces at Rye and Tenterden.

Full length films soon became the fare and on many occasions films were shown free of charge in the hope that they would interest young men into signing up for the Army — these were of general views of camp life and so on. Woman, girls and boys under 16 were barred from these events. Eventually it appears that Women and Children were barred from the cinema generally, which ended up in the Electric Palace being picketed by Suffragettes.

The Cinema burned to the ground at the height of the pickets in a mysterious fire — arson has not been ruled out.

The glow of the blaze that January evening was reported to have seen seen as far away as Eastbourne. The site is now occupied by Woolworths.

Elite 'All Talkie' — *see Elite Cinema*

Exterior shot of the Electric Palace, Wellington Place (1912) — The boats that are pictured, used to be pulled into the town centre because of high tides and extensive flooding to the sea-front.

Photographs of the big Electric Palace fire of January, 1915.

(21) Elite Cinema
Royal Terrace, Warrior Square, Central St. Leonards

Warrior Square Opera House and Concert Hall — Royal Concert Hall — Elite Picture Theatre — Elite 'All Talkie' — Union Cinemas Elite — Elite Cinema — Elite Super Theatre

CINEMA: 1921 - 40. 1942 (only). (1947)

The St. Leonards-on-sea Elite goes down in history as the unluckiest cinema in the United Kingdom. The building that eventually housed this ill-fated cinema began life on 13th October 1879 as the Warrior Square Opera House and Concert Hall.

It was built mainly of wood and had a seating capacity on one level for exactly 1,000 people and boasted an organ that had once graced Lichfield Cathedral. It later became the Royal Concert Hall.

At the turn of the century shows ended and were replaced by the new roller skating craze; this in turn was replaced by bicycling.

Stage returned on Wednesday, 13th March 1901, when a very young Winston Churchill gave a lecture on how he escaped from the Boers in a cattle truck.

The Royal Concert Hall became home to many a weird and wonderful concert — on one occasion there was barely a dry eye in the house when a capacity audience came along to see twenty pianists play ten upright pianos and on another occasion, again a full house, watched the Ore Choral Society perform their rendition of hymns.

It was at this time that people were into child prodigies in a big way and it was this infatuation that packed out the town's theatres and concert halls — however, on one fateful occasion a young prodigy was performing on Hastings Pier when the ladies in the audience began shrieking like guinea pigs and squawking like cockatiels and then persisted in bombing the poor child with nuts, apple cores, flour and water bombs. This particular scene outraged the Royal Concert Hall so much that they placed the following advertisement in the Hastings and St. Leonards Observer: 'We hope that the ladies will restrain their feelings on this occasion and that there will be no repetition of that foolish scene when little Florizel Von Reuter played his violen on Hastings Pier. How on earth a host of 'Well-bred' and 'Sensible' members of the fair sex can behave so badly as to mob a young musician is utterly beyond us. The screaming, in which we are sorry to say, even ladies of quality engaged, was hardly in keeping with the dulcet tones rendered by so gifted a child'.

Fortunately there was to be no repetition of the 1909 event. The Royal Concert Hall was abandoned in 1918 and remained derelict until 1921.

As 1921 dawned, the hall was taken over and transformed into a cinema. A circle was constructed, which gave the hall an extended capacity of 1,600. The Elite Picture Theatre opened at 6 pm on Monday, 14th March 1921, with *The Auction Mart.*

Talkies arrived in February 1930 when it was re-named the Elite All Talkie and occasionally Elite Talkie Theatre.

For the first 19 years luck shone down on the Elite, but luck was something that was soon to run out for the cinema. On Wednesday, 26th September 1940, the frontage of the Elite was badly damaged in a bombing raid, which totally flattened the adjacent church. Fortunately no one was killed and the only injuries were sustained by the doorman who was blown through the front doors.

After a £50,000 repair bill had been met, the Elite re-opened on Easter Monday 1942 with *Sullivan's Travels.*

Just six months later the Elite was again a wreck as it was half-destroyed in another bomb attack, this time during October 1942. Again there were no fatalities.

Once hostilities had ended, the undeterred proprietors set about repairing the cinema and after a £100,000 refit the Elite was again ready to welcome patrons.

An advertisement was placed in the Hastings & St. Leonards Observer which gave details of the first two programmes of the new Elite Super Cinema. It was set to re-open on Monday, 23rd June 1947 with *Wild Harvest*. The following week's attraction was to be *Blaze of Noon*.

Posters outside the cinema read: 'Our Next Presentation . . . At Great Expense to the Elite . . . *The Blaze of Noon*.' This was to be a bad omen for the cinema because on its re-opening day the cinema burst into flames and burned to the ground. All that remained were three outside walls with the 'At great Expense to the Elite . . . Blaze of Noon' posters. And yes, the fire naturally started at exactly noon!

By 12.10 pm flames were leaping over 50 feet in the air and by all accounts could be seen in France. The entire Borough was covered by a thick black cloud of smoke as the hot summer's day was turned into night. It is still looked upon as the biggest fire ever in St. Leonards.

The owners returned from lunch and as they watched helplessly a telegram arrived wishing them luck in their new venture.

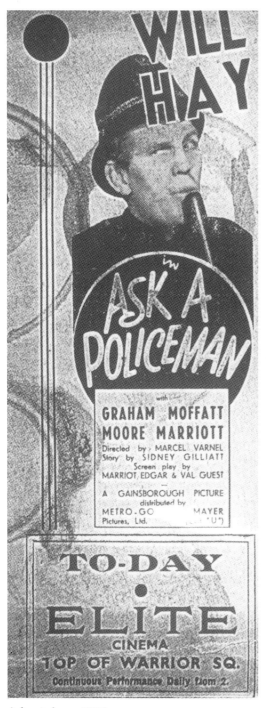

Advert from 1939.

A shot of an early queue.

A full house at the Royal Concert Hall during the Great War.

Sketch of Royal Concert Hall. (Note the grand organ, which came from Lichfield Cathedral).

A publicity campaign for *Oliver Twist* during the 1920s.

Sketch from *Hastings and St. Leonards Observer,* showing the Elite's new frontage (1932).

The Elite Cinema goes up in flames just hours before its opening (1947).

The Elite Cinema — the 1947 fire covered the entire Borough in thick smoke.

Monday, 23rd June 1947 will be remembered as the day that an entire town stopped in its tracks and rushed to the scene. By all accounts nearly a quarter of the population walked out of their jobs, trolley buses stopped and pubs closed because everyone was in Warrior Square. Within 20 minutes of the fire breaking out, some 5,000 people were in the square, ten minutes later the total is estimated as being 10,000 and as many as 15,000 crammed into St. Leonards to see what was happening.

The two families who owned the parent company, the Hastings Cinema Co., were the Segals and the Jays. Although they decided not to rebuild the ill-fated Elite again, they continued to run their other 18 cinemas, which included the De Luxe, Hastings. The Jays' famous son Peter continues to run the companies two surviving cinemas, both of which are in Great Yarmouth.

Arson was never ruled out. The site remained empty until the Royal Terrace warden-controlled flats opened in April 1986.

Elite Picture Theatre — *see Elite Cinema*
Elite Super Cinema — *see Elite Cinema*

---

(22) Eylseum
Drill Hall, Bank Buildings, Station Road, Town Centre, Hastings

CINEMA: 1911 (Only)

During March 1911 the Drill Hall was used for public film shows three days a week. Details of its programming policy can't be found but it is known that the seating wasn't fitted to the floor. It is obvious that the Eylseum couldn't compete with the Central Picture Theatre two doors away and was shut by January 1912.

Galaxy Seven Sex Cinema Club — *see Orion Cinema*

---

(23) Grand Cinema
American Palace Pier (St. Leonards Pier - shore end), Marina, St. Leonards-on-sea

Jury's Imperial Pictures — Imperial Cinema — Grand Electric Theatre — Grand Cinema

CINEMA: 1907 - 13

ADVERTISING SLOGAN: *The Greatest Picture House of its kind in existence.*

St. Leonards Pier, later American Palace Pier and Palace Pier opened in 1881.

Film shows arrived here in the shore end hall during 1898 and became more regular with the arrival of Jury's Imperial Pictures which were screened for five days a week.

The opening attractions were headed by a film entitled *Canadian Life,* which was all about tree felling, wheat harvesting and salmon fishing. The programme concluded with some entertainment supplied by Dr. Seaton and Professor Trillo, who were renowned for their conjuring and ventriloquism.

Films were generally shown for the entire high season from 1907 onwards, the last of which was in 1913. The St. Leonards Pier came to an abrupt end on Friday, 8th October 1940, when it was devastated by a huge bomb. It was never repaired and spent the remainder of the war in three bits, which were demolished in 1951, while a few traces of the Pier remain in the form of stumps amongst the shingle.

---

(24) Granville

St, Georges Road, West Hill, Hastings

CINEMA: 1911

Another litte-know film venue was the Granville Hotel, which presented films on alternate Friday and Saturday nights during the Summer of 1911 under the control of the landlord. The films were shown in what is now the function room.

---

(25) Haggar's Royal Electric Bioscope

Priory Meadow, Town Centre, Hastings

CINEMA: 1902 (Only)

Haggar's Royal Electric Bioscope was a mobile cinema which was operated inside a caravan that was similar in size to a Gypsy Caravan.

Haggar's Royal Electric Bioscope, Priory Meadow, Hastings in 1902. Photo taken prior to its arrival in the Borough.

Haggar's was part of Barnham and Bailey's Circus, which came to Priory Meadow through the high season of 1902. When the circus left town, the Bioscope show was doing such great trade that it stayed until that October when Harry Furniss started his cinemas in the Old Town.

---

(26) Hastings Pier Cinema Theatre

Hastings Pier, White Rock, Hastings

Hastings Pier was opened to the public circa 1862 and went on to screen its first film some 36 years later. The occasional film shows continued until the Hastings Pier Cinema Theatre opened in 1911.

Its opening film on Monday, 13th March 1911, was *The Cult of the Dahlia,* a film that showed the cultivation of that well-known flower. A week later the Hastings and St. Leonards Observer reported: 'Two hours can be spent at the Hastings Pier very pleasantly and profitably. The pictures continue to attract large numbers of animated picture lovers in the afternoons and evenings.'

Films generally took a break during the winter months when stage took over. The cinema closed at the end of the 1914 high season and never again re-opened although occasional films were presented until the late 1930s. It is currently the Pier Bingo club.

Hippodrome — *see De Luxe Cinema*
Imperial Cinema — *see Grand Cinema*
Imperial Cinematograph Co. — *see Bohemia Electric Theatre*
Jury's Imperial Pictures — *see Grand Cinema*
Kinema — *see Bulverhythe Kinema*
Kinema — *see Curzon*
Kinema — *see St. Leonards Kinema*
Kinema Palace — *see Curzon*
Kinema World — *see Saxon*

---

(27) The Kinetoscope
41 Robertson Street, Town Centre, Hastings

OPEN: 1895 - 98

SLOGAN: *Living Pictures of a new order!*

It was on Monday, 19th January 1895, that the first moving film was presented to a paying public in the Borough — although the Kinetoscope didn't use a projector or a screen.

The Edison Kinetoscope was a large wooden box, very similar to a What the Butler Saw machine, with the exception that it ran off electricity and used 35mm film instead of photographs.

During the first afternoon of business the Hastings Kinetoscope, which was believed to have been the first outside London, was visited by a Hastings and St. Leonards Observer reporter and the following report appeared in the next edition; 'Those who would see the latest wonderful production of electricity should pay a visit to No. 41 Robertson Street, and patronise the Kinetoscope, the invention of that colossal genius, T. A. Edison.

'The machine is indeed a perfect marvel. Looking through the wonderful machine, we see a production of life in action, not in repose, or posing, but the actual doings, for instance, in a barber's shop, or a bar, or the graceful evolutions of a dancer. These pictures are the result of a contrivance in which photography and electricity are combined.

'We saw a dancer performing the butterfly dance, someone going through his exercises, and an incident in a bar. In this last we saw a man come in and order a drink. He was followed by others, and summarily ejected from the premises, every detail being complete. There are also other pictures.'

The Kinetoscope survived in the basement until the Piers both started film programmes in 1898. It is currently a hairdresser's.

---

(28) Kino de Bo Peep

Seaside Road, Bo Peep, St. Leonards-on-sea

CINEMA: 1912 (Only)

Another very very short-lived cinema was the Kino de Bo Peep, which operated in a private house somewhere in Seaside Road. It was shut by December 1912.

---

(29) Kosmos Kinema

Priory Road, West Hill, Hastings

CINEMA: 1912 - 13

Hardly anything is known about this picture palace other than the fact that it was situated on Priory Road, between Halton and the West Hill, near the old Fire Station.

---

(30) La Dolce Vita Sex Cinema Club

Dolphin Bingo Club, Marine Court, Marina, St. Leonards-on-sea

CINEMA: 1971 (Only)

During 1971, the Dolphin Bingo Club was transformed into a luxury sex cinema called La Dolce Vita. Each programme consisted of entirely uncensored Continental feature films. The club opened six nights a week (except Sunday) and had two nightly screenings with a weekly change of programme.

Admission could only be gained by members and other than the cinema's opening advertisement, it never again advertised in the press.

John Sutherland was General Manager and La Dolce Vita opened with the hard-core movie *Flesh*. Only weeks earlier police raided a six cinema in London and snatched a copy of the film shortly after its British premiere. Other seedy offerings were booked some months ahead. La Dolce Vita wasn't a success and shut very quietly at the end of 1971.

The opening announcement of what was to be the town's only hard porn club.

Marine Theatre of Varieties — *see De Luxe Cinema*

---

(31) Market Hall Kinema
Lower Market Hall, George Street, Old Town, Hastings

CINEMA: 1907 - 09

The lower Market Hall in George Street was occasionally used for public films although details are few. In 1909 the venue was used for the last time when the Victoria Cinema opened in the upper Market Hall.

---

(32) New Golden Cross Kinema
Havelock Road, Town Centre, Hastings

CINEMA: (Circa) 1911

The New Golden Cross Public House (Now Old Golden Cross) operated film shows in its function room.

---

(33) Norman Kinema
Veruliam Place, Eversfield Place, White Sea Front, St. Leonards-on-sea

CINEMA: 1912 (Only)

A small cinema opened in the basement of Gasson's Marine Stores and only survived for a few months during 1912. During the 1960s and 70s the site was used as a car park and a block of sheltered flats now stands on the site.

Odeon — *see Orion Cinema*

(Proposed) Odeon Cinema
London Road, St. Leonards-on-sea

In 1935, the Odeon cinema chain put forward plans to build a 3,500 seat super cinema on Gensing Gardens. At a later date the plan was dropped and to date there has never been an Odeon in the area.

---

(34) Old Town Kinema
All Saints Street, Old Town, Hastings

CINEMA: 1909 (Only)

A first-floor area of East Cliff House (see East Cliff Electric Bioscope), was used as a cinema. It was closed within a year and in more recent years has been Capel's night club. The area is currently derelict.

Open Air Cinema(s) (35) Alexandra Park
(36) West Hill
(37) White Rock

CINEMA(S): 1912 (Only)

A very peculiar format of cinema exhibition took place at three different locations in the Borough. The Open Air Cinema(s) operated six days a week and showed films for eight hours a day. The idea became extremely short-lived. The seating was in the form of benches and the screen was a sheet on which images were rear projected. See map for exact locations.

Original Silverhill Cinema — *see Silverhill Cinema Complex*

---

(38) Orion Cinema
Robertson Street, Town Centre, Hastings

People's Public Hall — Public Hall — Public Hall Cinema — Plaza All Talkie — Plaza Talkie Theatre — Plaza Cinema — Orion Cinema

CINEMA: 1913 - 78

NICK NAME: *The Urinal*

NAME PRONOUNCED: 1948 - 62 Or'E'on 1962 - 78 Or'I'on

The Public Hall Assembly Rooms were built in 1875 and part of it in those days was occupied by Cole and Rossiters School of Science and Art.

Magic Lantern shows were given in the early 1890s and occasional films arrived in 1902 although it would be another 11 years until the Public Hall would become a full time cinema.

The Public Hall Cinema opened on 24th July 1913, with a gala charity opening, when the first day's take, a princely £17 was donated to the East Sussex Hospital.

Admission was 3d, 6d, and 1/- and the films were accompanied by an organ, built at St. Mary's Terrace; the instrument could be played as an organ or piano or, when desired, both together!

According to a lecture by Barry Funnel, the 3d seats were occupied by orange-pip spitters and apple-core chuckers, who made the poor organist's life hell as he became the target of their misdemeanours. It was quite common for him to crash down on the keys and physically remove the offenders from the cinema.

In 1930 the old silent cinema was acquired by Miss Dorothy Meatyard. She immediately closed the Public Hall Cinema and ordered it to be scrubbed with strong disinfectant in the hope of killing off the fleas. The old movie house re-opened as the Plaza 'All Talkie'.

During March 1937 the cinema was again refurbished, when a new sound system, seats and projectors were installed.

Tragedy hit on Monday, 30th September 1940 when a bomb struck the facade. Fourteen people were killed, including the manager, who was chatting outside. Twelve others were seriously injured.

The Cranfield Cinema Co. took over in 1948 and re-named the Plaza the Orion, the name that the cinema would keep for its remaining 30 years.

Cranfield had a plan of selling their cinemas to the Odeon circuit. They started by using the traditional square ODEON lettering in their adverts and went so far as to pronounce Orion as Or'E'on, which is the pronounciation that most locals still use when recalling the cinema. Whilst Odeon were interested in this particular cinema and the Silverhill Roxy, they were not too keen on the Orions at Midhurst, Burgess Hill or Hassocks. The deal eventually fell through.

The People's Public Hall at the turn of the century.

As the Public Hall Cinema during the silent days.

This newspaper photo shows the complete devastation caused by the bomb (1940).

Manager Fred Heppell, who was
killed in the Plaza bomb outrage (1940).

As the Orion Cinema in October 1977. A year later it would be in the process of being gutted.

Bill Grant Theatres took over in 1962. It was now that the musicals, westerns and classic movies made way for more sleezy offerings. In 1970 Grant signed a new eight-year lease but not before there was a fight with a group of Mormons who wanted to use the Orion as their meeting house.

The following year the Orion announced that it was to become the Galaxy 7 Sex Cinema Club, which would show uncensored movies only. The reason for this move was to compete with La Dolce Vita at Marine Court, St. Leonards. But before the Orion could see its plans materialise La Dolce Vita was shut, so the dear old Orion remained a public cinema.

During the mid 1970s the Orion upset a few people with its attractions; these included some Scouts and an Irish religious organisation who cancelled holidays to Hastings because of the Orion.

In 1976 the remainder of the Orion's lease was sold to Supercharge Ltd, who, under the guidance of Don Smith Enterprises Ltd., ran the Penguin Cinema in Priory Street. Jeff Ing, who was formerly manager at the Penguin, moved round the corner to the Orion.

At a massive auction at the Queens Hotel in October 1977, the row of property that included the cinema, York and Crypt bars, W. H. Smith and Jax Fashions was sold for £250,000. It had been owned by the Central Assembly Room and Arcade Co. for 102 years.

The programming policy changed dramatically at the Orion for the 1978 summer season as first-run sex films were dropped and replaced by family orientated films such as *Star Wars, Viva Kineval, ABBA - The Movie, The Spy Who Loved Me, Spiderman - The Movie, Sky Divers* and so on.

Although rumours were circulating that the Orion was on its death bed, it enjoyed success from its new family audience, most of whom had been acquired from the recently closed Curzon in Norman Road.

During the summer of '78 it was announced that W. H. Smith had purchased the freehold of the block and intended to extend their small ground-floor shop into the cinema and make a larger store.

The 544-seater continued to pack them in and was indeed making a profit, not only from the cinema, but also from their Super 8 Film Library which ran along the lines that a video shop does today. At the height of the summer season, W. H. Smith had plans passed for their new store and work was to commence once the cinema lease had expired from 1st September.

However, as the final month drew to a close there was a ray of hope because the Classic in Queens Road was in negotiation with Tesco who wanted to expand their store into that cinema. The Council got involved and decided that should the Classic close they would rescind planning permission to Smiths. It has never been publicly announced whether Smiths were ever prepared to negotiate with the Orion for a new lease anyway.

The irony of the situation is that although the Orion was making money it was faced with the prospect of only getting one film in five first run, with the Classic getting the other four, so with the recent arrival of video it seemed no point to play second run. What is even more ironic is that

The Orion site today.

That's all folks! — Due to expiry of lease, the profit making Orion closed down on 31st August 1978, a move that left the Borough with just one film venue.

less than ten years later the unfair cinema release barring system would be dissolved so that the Orion would have been able to get the Odeon release, with the Classic playing Classic and ABC release.

Hastings Council forced Classic to make a snap decision as to whether they were to close or not! The decision was made and the Classic stayed open. The poor old Orion would be shut in less than two weeks time.

The house-lights were dipped at the Orion for the last time at 8.25 pm on Thursday, 31st August 1978, for a very busy performance of *Star Wars*.

The Orion had been a cinema for 65 years and even to this day enjoyed a longer cinema life than any other Hastings Picture House, though the Cannon (Classic) will beat this record in March 1997.

Attempts were made by two cinema operators to take over the Orion, one of them from the Channel Islands, but it was all too late and W. H. Smith opened their extended store in 1979.

---

(39) Orion Preview Cinema
Veruliam Place, Eversfield Place, Sea Front, St. Leonards-on-sea

Following the closure of the town centre Orion Cinema, Super Charge Ltd. transferred business to Eversfield Place, where they ran their Super 8 Home Movie shop. According to a newspaper report it would include a 40-seat preview cinema.

When video became big, the Super 8 Library was replaced by Orion Video, who ran video hire shops in Kings Road and Queens Road until the late 1980s. The Eversfield Place premises is currently occupied by Backyard.

---

(40) Palace Cinema
American Palace, (St. Leonards Pier - sea end), Marina, St. Leonards-on-sea

Palace Pier Electric Cinema — Palace Cinema

CINEMA: 1912 - 14

A second cinema opened on St. Leonards Pier during the first week of January 1912 and continued until that October. It then ran from March to October in 1913 and 1914 after which it closed.

See also Grand Cinema.

Palacette — *see Pelham Palacette*

---

(41) Pavilion Cinema
Pier Pavilion, Hastings Pier, White Rock, Hastings

CINEMA: 1913 - 14

The second cinema to operate on Hastings Pier was in the Pavilion which opened in January 1913 and closed that October. The 500-seater came back to life in March 1914 and shut for good that August. The Pavilion Cinema buildings was destroyed in the massive 1917 Hastings Pier Fire. The building that has more recently been used for Quasar and the Pier Discos replaced it. Coasters Disco now occupies the site.

Pelham Arcadian — *see Arcadian*
Pelham Hall — *see Pelham Palacette*
Pelham Hall Electric Theatre — *see Pelham Palacette*

---

(42) Pelham Palacette
Pelham Arcade, Pelham Place, Old Town, Hastings

Pelham Hall Assembly Room — Pelham Hall Electric Theatre — Pelham Palacette

CINEMA: 1909 - 17

ADVERTISING SLOGAN: *Hastings Prettiest and Most Comfortable Bijou Picture resort.*

What was originally thought to have been Hastings' first full-time cinema was converted from the old Pelham Hall Assembly Room which was situated in the Pelham Arcade. It was built in 1780 and was used for all types of popular entertainment. Occasional film shows started in 1905 and by 1909 were proving to be so popular that all other forms of entertainment were dropped.

When it became clear that at least four other cinemas were shortly to open within half a mile of the Hall, the owners immediately started a refurbishment programme.

The Pelham Hall Electric Theatre was officially opened on Wednesday, 1st June 1910. Admission was 3d and 6d for adults and 2d and 3d for children. There was also a special reduction for schools.

Messrs. Lane, Daly and Lane, were the proprietors of whom Mr. T. C. Daly was manager. It was Daly who made the venture a success as he put his heart and soul into it.

Daly staged many amazing fund-raising events, when the entire day's take was given to worthy causes — among these was free shows for local disadvantaged children and workhouse inmates, all of whom had been sponsored by local institutions or businesses.

Another popular event was staged when Mr. Daly gave away £160 in cash prizes for the best essay on the Daily Mail film *From Forest to Breakfast Table,* a movie that showed the entire process of producing a newspaper from the tree being cut down through to the paper being delivered to the front door.

Shortly after this, Daly booked the film *Jes - Plain Dog* to which the director added the following line, 'This picture is in fond memory of my beloved dog Jes, who alone has been more faithful to me than any one of my six wives.'

Obviously no one was more shocked than Daly when hordes of women, among them several hundred Suffragettes, picketed the cinema in an attempt to get the film banned. The appeal failed and the film continued its run playing to full houses all week.

Why Daly, Lane & Daly should want to sell the cinema will always remain a mystery but Edward Van Biene and George C. Child took over the lease during early 1912 and closed the cinema for a modernisation programme which included brand new tip-up seating, projectors and general fittings, which now included screen curtains and carpets.

The cinema re-opened on Saturday, 6th April 1912, as the Pelham Palacette (Palacette meaning small Palace). The Palacette retained the theatre's policy of fund raising and less than three weeks after its re-opening, the entire day's take was given to the Lord Mayor of London's Titanic appeal.

Licensing laws forbade cinemas to operate on a Sunday back in those days, so from September 1913 the Rev. Mostyn Pinnock hired the cinema twice on Sundays for evangelistic services.

By 1915 though the nearby 2,300 seat Royal Cinema De Luxe had taken its stranglehold on the 500-seat Pelham Palacette, which by now had engulfed the Pelham Arcadian Cinema too.

Attendances continued to decline over the next two years, but despite this, Child still continued to raise funds for the Red Cross and other such needy organisations.

The Pelham Hall Electric Theatre, Hastings — with inmates of the old Hastings Workhouse.

According to a lecture by Barry Funnel, during the Palacette's dying days, Colin MacDougal, Hastings' first inspector of cinemas and Chief Fire Officer for the Borough, sat behind the screen during the film *Highland Pipers* and played the bagpipes in a last ditch desperate attempt to get people to attend the hall although it isn't certain how many people attended this 'attraction' but sure enough, as recent returns for the cinema had predicted, the cinema went bankrupt sometime during 1917.

Since those days part of the old cinema has been used as a Wimpy Bar and now forms part of the Out of this World Leisure Complex. The remainder of the old Palacette remains dormant behind a row of fish restaurants, shops, and amusement arcades waiting to be re-discovered after eight decades with the formation of the St. Mary's Art Centre development. *(see St. Mary's Art Centre).*

As the Pelham Palacette, showing wounded soldiers and nurses from the long defunct Hospital of St. John, Holmesdale Gardens, Hastings.

(43) Penguin Cinema

Priory Street, Town Centre, Hastings

Women's Institute — Casino Bingo Club — Priory Street Bingo — Penguin Cinema — Penguin Snooker

CINEMA: 1974 - 77

ADVERTISING SLOGAN: *If some of our scenes get a little too hot for you, why not cool off in our bar.*

Following the closure of the ABC Ritz in 1971, Don Smith Enterprises Ltd. decided to turn the upper level of their bingo club in Priory Street into a cinema — the plans for the town's first public cinema for 35 years were passed on Tuesday, 25th September 1973.

Two days later, Don Smith (a former De Luxe projectionist) told the long defunct *Hastings and St. Leonards Herald:* 'We feel that Hastings lacks cinemas now that the ABC and others have gone (though the Classic 1 & 2, Orion, and Curzon, St. Leonards still survived) and by introducing a cinema here we will be making full use of the building already covered on its overheads by a paying business so we feel we really can't lose.' Why the cinema closed some 2½ years after opening remains a mystery — but like Mr. Smith, I too have made statements about opening cinemas in the area and why they should work, but alas, they always fail.

The cinema took 18 months to build because work could only take place during the night once the bingo sessions had ended. It took 25 tons of concrete, six tons of steel and £20,000 before the Penguin Cinema was ready to welcome its first 200 customers.

How the *Hastings Observer* announced the Penguin Cinema's arrival in August, 1974.

The cinema that at the outset planned to show 75% family films opened on Sunday, 24th August 1974 with the classic film, *The Guns of Navarone*.

In those early days the Penguin screened late night shows on weekend evenings and had a Saturday morning Cinema Club — but sadly these ideas were unsupported and were dropped.

The Penguin soon found that it was playing third run, and if the Orion sex cinema wanted to get involved with a major film, the Penguin would have fourth-run films.

Soon after this the Penguin went over to second-run sex. This was reflected in its newspaper adverts which read, 'If some of our scenes get a little too hot for you then why not cool off in our bar?'

The Summer of 1976 was certainly a cool one for the Penguin, often without a single soul turning out for a film.

As 1977 dawned the Penguin became the first Hastings cinema to go over to part-time opening (evenings only) and during the second week of January 1977 the Penguin bolted its doors after a screening of *Confessions of a Sexy Photographer*. The film didn't even end its seven-day run.

Apparently the Penguin had only closed for the remainder of the winter — but it's been a long winter, which has now lasted some 19 years.

At one time there were plans to re-open the Penguin as a twin, with a brand new 300-seat Penguin Cinema opening in the old Paxman Press building which was adjacent (demolished second week of March 1996) and the present 200-seater would be Penguin Two. The plans were quietly dropped along with the bingo club and the entire Penguin complex enjoys a successful life as the Penguin Snooker Club, with the basement leased out to Dennies Nightclub.

———————

People's Public Hall — *see Orion Cinema*
Picturedrome — *see Bohemia Picturedrome*
Picture House — *see Roxy*
Plaza 'All Talkie' — *see Orion Cinema*
Plaza Talkie Theatre — *see Orion Cinema*
Princess Cinema — *see Cynthia*
Public Hall Cinema — *see Orion Cinema*

———————

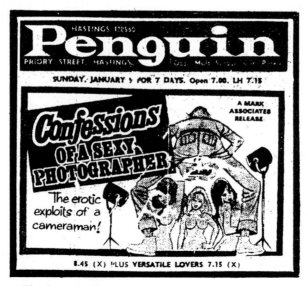

Final advert for the short-lived Penguin (1977).

(44) Regal Cinema
London Road and Kings Road, Central St. Leonards-on-sea

Regal Super Theatre — Union Cinemas Regal — Regal — Regal Cinema — ABC Regal

CINEMA: 1932 - 56

At the turn of this century it was said that the steep hill that overlooked Warrior Square Station from the London Road direction was impossible to be developed.

Despite this, some 32 years later Union Cinemas started to build the town's first super cinema. John B. Mendham was the architect and a Mr. Harvey constructed the cinema of over one million bricks from the nearby Bexhill Brickworks.

The Regal, London Road, St. Leonards-on-sea.

It was at exactly 8 pm on Saturday, 6th August 1932, that the manager, Mr. E. V. Delorme, unlocked the doors for the first time — he was formerly the manager at the nearby Elite.

The opening attraction was *Jack's the Boy* starring Jack Hulbert. The supporting programme included a newsreel, a song-recital film with Richard Tauber and organ interludes given by the late Gerald Shaw (who committed suicide in the mid-1970s) on the 'Mighty Regal Organ', a three-manual instrument manufactured by John Compton.

There was a tiny entrance that led off the footpath by Warrior Square Station, whilst the main entrance was graced by a grand facade on the London Road.

This unique cinema had a circle built at ground level to the main entrance while a series of short flights of stairs led to the stalls. The total seating capacity was 1,616.

Three shots of the derelict Regal,
just prior to demolition in April 1973.

A large dome, which was set in the ceiling above the balcony, was fitted with hidden lights, which provided the majority of the light to the whole hall, while some smaller lights were fitted on the side walls.

The entire building had an unlimited supply of hot water, which was the first time that many of its pre-war patrons had washed their hands under hot water without previously having to boil a kettle. Above the cloakrooms were commodious tea rooms and lounges which were even fitted with a soda fountain.

Green and silver was the colour scheme that was fitted throughout the building. A vast screen was situated at the rear of the massive stage, behind which were 16 dressing rooms — The Regal Super Theatre was well accepted by locals because of the recent demise of the Gaiety Theatre in Queens Road, which was being converted into a cinema.

All through the 1930s, film and stage worked hand in hand. The first show was given by the Hastings Players, who were followed in quick succession by the latest and greatest names in the world of showbusiness. These included Louis Armstrong, Duke Ellington and top bands like those of Jack Hylton and Jack Payne.

During the same period of time the Union Cinemas' Chums Club was held every Saturday morning. This ended at the end of 1937 when Union Cinemas went bust.

The Regal Super Theatre closed in 1940 and remained closed for the remainder of the war. It re-opened in 1946 as the Regal Cinema, solely for film. This policy changed in 1950 when it became the ABC Regal. From now on shows ran for the high season while films ran for the winter.

Many top names appeared at the Regal. These included Jessie Matthews, who appeared in *Private Lives,* and the Lyons Family, who paid a highly successful visit to promote their latest film *Life with the Lyons.* Eileen Joyce, the pianist, was another visitor and in 1955 the Carl Rose Opera Co. had a most successful week.

Throughout the eighteen years that it was open, the Regal never made a profit and in September 1956 the decision was taken to close it down. The final show starred the famous stripper Miss Phyllis Dixie, while the last film was *Destination Gobi,* which was screened on Saturday, 8th September 1956. It is widely believed that the St. Leonards Regal was the first victim of television in an area that wasn't served by an ITV company. It would be another two years before Southern Television started broadcasting.

By the end of that month the Regal was all but a shell as eager workmen ripped the place apart. Shortly after closure it was used for one final time, when Syncopating Sandy broke the world piano-playing record, which earned him a place in the Guinness book of records for the next 26 years.

The Regal, which is believed to have been the first cinema to have been fitted with a loop hearing system for the deaf, remained empty until 1973, when it was demolished in order to make way for the twelve-storey Gundolphus House, which was completed in 1975. It is now called Ocean House.

Originally the Regal was to have another name and although this has been a mystery for the past 64 years, I can hold my head up high and announce that according to recently discovered plans, which I now have in my possession, it was to have been the Rialto.

Ritz Cinema — *see ABC*

---

(45) Roebuck Inn

High Street, Old Town, Hastings

In 1890 the Roebuck Inn regularly presented magic lantern shows and on a couple of occasions, films were presented too. It closed later that year and Roebuck Street now runs through the site of the old Inn.

Royal Cinema De Luxe — *see Deluxe Cinema*

---

(46) Royal George

Station Road and Devonshire Road, Town Centre, Hastings

CINEMA: 1912 (Only)

Another public house that occasionally showed films was the Royal George which formed a 170-seater in its first-floor function room. It had ceased operating by December 1912.

---

(47) Roxy Cinema

London Road, Silverhill, St. Leonards-on-sea

Silverhill Picture House — Roxy Cinema — Roxy Continental — Roxy Cinema

CINEMA: 1913 - 60

ADVERTISING SLOGAN: *We're the house of quantity, quality and comfort.*

The Silverhill Picture House opened on 29th November 1913, on a site that had previously been occupied by the Clarence Nurseries.

Back in those very early days the Silverhill Picture Palace concentrated mainly on cine-variety. This format continued until 1930 when Miss Dorothy Meatyard took over and re-named it the Roxy.

It was during this era that the Roxy had an attendant walk around with a deodorant spray and cover the entire place with the strange substance — while this was taking place a slide appeared on screen which read: 'This house is now being sprayed with June.'

Another one bites the dust — The Roxy, Silverhill, nine years after closure, shortly before demolition in 1969.

A trolley bus passes the Roxy (year unknown).

A programme for both of the Borough's Cranfield Cinemas —
The Orion at Hastings and the Roxy at Silverhill.

Meatyard sold the Roxy to the Cranfield Cinema Co. in 1948 and when attendances started to fall it was transformed into the Roxy Continental. *An Artist with the Ladies* (X) was the first attraction. By 1959 it was again called The Roxy but still continued with an art-house booking policy, with names such as Felini and Jacques Tati playing to full houses.

In 1960, Cranfield received a large offer from a development company to sell the Roxy. It was an offer that Cranfield couldn't refuse and, despite again making a profit, the Roxy closed on Saturday, 30th April 1960, after a screening of *Mogambo.*

The cinema then stood empty for the next nine years when it was eventually demolished in September 1969. Carpetland now occupies the site of the old 450-seater.

Roxy Continental — *see Roxy Cinema*

(48) St. Leonards Kinema
Norman Road, Central St. Leonards-on-sea

CINEMA: 1912 (Only)

Another long forgotten cinema was the St. Leonards Kinema which was situated on the junction of Norman Road and Western Road in what is now the derelict Marlborough Hotel Complex.

A sketch of Pelham Place and Pelham Crescent, shows St. Mary in the Castle, soon to be St. Mary's Art Centre.

Interior of the St. Mary's Art Centre (1995).

(49) St. Mary's Art Centre
Pelham Crescent, Old Town, Hastings

CINEMA: Possibly from 1997

The historic Regency church that is the centre-piece of the art-deco Pelham Crescent is currently undergoing a multi-million pound restoration programme that will eventually see it being transformed into a 600-seat arts venue, with cinema, theatre, exhibitions and music.

The Friends of St. Mary in the Castle (F.O.S.M.I.C.) have recently been granted a £1.3m cash grant from the National Lottery to aid them as they transform the council-owned building.

---

(50) Saxon Cinema
Junction Saxon Road and Old London Road, Christchurch, Ore Village, Hastings

CINEMA: 1912 (Only)

Another tiny cinema was the Saxon which was the first of Ore's two cinemas. Its auditorium was situated on the first floor. It operated between August and December 1912 and is now the Nationwide Building Society.

Silverhill Cinema Complex
Sedlescombe Road South, Silverhill, St. Leonards-on-sea

(51) Silverhill Cinema — *later Original Silverhill Cinema*
(52) Silverhill Cinema
(53) Silverhill Palace

CINEMA(S): 1912 - 22

ADVERTISING SLOGAN: (51) Silverhill Cinema
Come and see Us — we are the only cinema in Silverhill that is showing PICTURES only!

The busy Silverhill junction at one time boasted FOUR cinemas. These were the Silverhill Cinema, Original Silverhill Cinema, Silverhill Palace and Silverhill Picture House.

At this point I'm quite sure that you are totally confused!

The first Silverhill Cinema opened on the top floor of the old Assembly Rooms, which were completed in 1894.

All went well for the first eighteen months until the Silverhill Picture House opened opposite (see Roxy). There was some very stiff marketing going on in the local press and eventually the former closed.

On Monday, 19th July 1915, the Silverhill Cinema came back to life as the Original Silverhill Cinema. Less than three months later the ground floor of the Silverhill Assembly Rooms opened as the short-lived Silverhill Cinema. The new cinema with this name had a separate entrance from its brother upstairs and lasted for less than a year. However prior to its demise a third cinema opened in December 1915 called the Silverhill Palace. This became the last cinema to open in Silverhill and, despite having a different name, it used the same entrance and set of stairs as the (upstairs) Original Silverhill Cinema, but had a different pay desk, which was situated adjacent to its auditorium above the old Chemist.

The last two cinemas were shut by the end of the summer of 1916 and the Original Silverhill Cinema was reduced to offering free tea and biscuits at all performances. This policy failed and the cinema again closed.

The Original Cinema came briefly back to life in 1918 and again in 1921. It closed for the last time during February 1922, when it became the Palais de Danse. Both floors are now occupied by the Silverhill Club, where apparently the portholes of the Original Cinema are still visible.

The single door on the left-hand side served the Silverhill Cinema. The double door on the right-hand side served the Silverhill Cinema/Original Silverhill Cinema (first floor) and the Silverhill Palace situated above the chemist. Just for the record, the old traffic lights were replaced by E. C. regulation lights (with white band around the side) in November 1978.

The 1986 16mm film season at the Stables Theatre, Hastings.

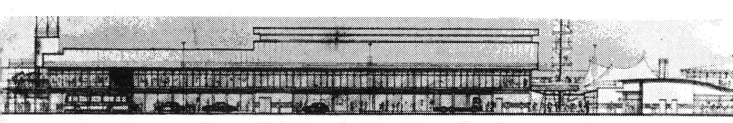

The proposed development for the Stade.

(54) Stables Theatres and Art Gallery
High Street and The Bourne, Old Town, Hastings

Sir Ralph Richardson officially opened the Stables Theatre in June 1959. The building was originally a stable block which was built in the 18th century by John Collier.

In 1975, a £65,000 extension appeal was launched and two years later work started on constructing a brand new entrance off The Bourne and a new bar and Art Gallery. It was completed in 1978.

Over the years the 160-seat two-tier theatre has gone from strength to strength and is now well-patronised by fringe theatre lovers from all over the region. In the early 1980s 16mm film shows started — these were of art-house films. The last of these was shown in 1993.

---

(55) Stade Development
The Stade, Old Town, Hastings

A plan to bring a £5m fun complex to the Stade, Hastings Sea Front, has at present been shelved until further notice. The plan includes restaurants, shops, water rides, helter-skelter and umpteen other attractions, which include the return of trams to the town for the first time since 1928 and a single-screen cinema. The problem at the present time seems to be that nobody like the design of the proposed 3½ acre complex, which has been described as 'Looking like Dungeness Power Station'. Part of the site will be built on top of an old Elizabethan Harbour.

---

(56) Swan Assembly Hall
Swan Hotel, High Street, Old Town, Hastings

The Swan Hotel enjoyed the second longest period of time as a Hastings hostelry. It was open for over 400 years. In the last century the Assembly room was all but rebuilt and it was here that the Borough's first magic lantern shows were given as early as 1875. Some 30 years earlier it has been

25 were killed when the Swan was bombed on Sunday 23rd March, 1943.

noted that over a hundred locals paid good money to see a shadow show. Between 1903 and 1914, films were occasionally shown to a paying public.

The Swan was destroyed in a raid on Sunday, 23rd May 1943 when 25 people were killed. A garden of remembrance now occupies part of the site.

Union Cinema de Luxe — *see De Luxe Cinema*
Union Cinemas Elite — *see Elite Cinema*
Union Cinemas Regal — *see Regal Cinema*

---

(57) Victoria Cinema
Upper Market Hall, George Street, Old Town, Hastings

CINEMA: 1909 - 10

In 1794, the old Rose and Crown Inn had its licence refused and after standing empty for many years it was demolished to make way for a Market Hall.

The foundation stone was laid by the blind Prince George of Cumberland in April 1933. The hall on the first floor became an Assembly Room, and, like all of its rivals, became used for every type of entertainment and in 1909 it became the Victoria Cinema, which survived until March 1910 — a victim of the 1910 Cinematograph Act. During the 1980s, it was Il Boccolino and it is now the George Street Hall. In recent years it has been used as a venue for 16mm art-house films. These ended very abruptly in 1994 because the hall didn't have a cinematograph licence, the very same reason that it closed down as a cinema in 1910.

Vogue — *see Curzon*

---

(58) Warrior Kinema
Warrior Square, Central St. Leonards-on-sea

For a very brief period in 1912 the Warrior Hotel screened films — the Hotel has been transformed into luxury apartments in more recent years.

---

(59) Wellington Kinema
York Buildings, Town Centre, Hastings

CINEMA: 1911 - 12

Very little is known about this old cinema, but it operated on the first floor of the grand looking building on the junction of Albert Road and York Buildings. For many years it has been used as offices for the Prudential, with the ground floor now being occupied by Q.S.

White Rock Pavilion — *See White Rock Theatre*

Interior of the White Rock Theatre (1985).

Exterior of White Rock Theatre (1987).

(60) White Rock Theatre
White Rock, Hastings

White Rock Pavilion — White Rock Theatre

The White Rock Pavilion was opened in 1927 by the Duke of Windsor. The 1,100+ seat Pavilion was used mainly for shows, although it held a cinema licence from 1927 to 1986 with films being presented on occasions from 1933 to 1977. In 1985 it was transformed into the White Rock Theatre after a staggering £1.3m was spent on it.

(61) *(Proposed Multiplex)*
White Rock Gardens, Hastings

At the time that this book was going to press, proposals had been put through to build a multi-purpose leisure complex on White Rock Gardens. The complex will include a leisure pool, numerous bars and restaurants, car parking, bingo, the areas second bowling alley, nightclub and a multiplex cinema with between 6 and 10 screens, depending on which operator signs up for the site. It is known that at least one multiplex operator has shown interest in the scheme.

The new Lib-Dem council has voted against the development of a Multiplex and will not pursue the idea whilst they have control. It had been given the seal of approval at a previous council meeting earlier this year (1996).

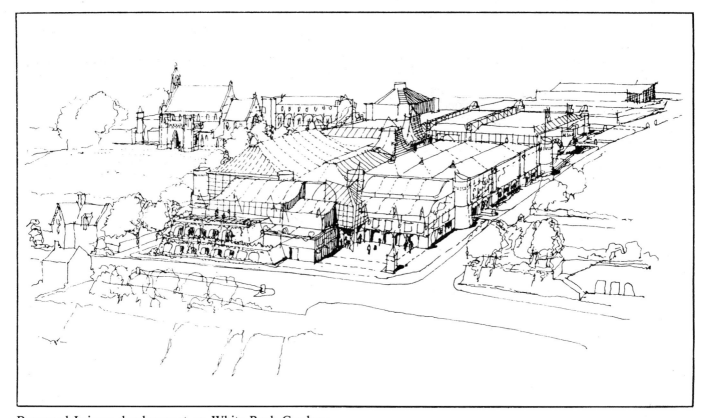

Proposed Leisure development on White Rock Gardens.

(62) *(Proposed Cinema)*
St. Leonards

The new Lib-Dem council has appled for a £12.5m government grant to help improve the Borough. One of the ideas for investment is a new cinema somewhere in St. Leonards. 15.6.96.

Some Hastings & St. Leonards-on-sea Notables

BALL, Nicholas .... Actor — played the Cockney Detective, Hazel.

BALL, Kevin .... Footballer — captain of Sunderland F.C.

BEANEY, Christopher .... Actor — starred in *Upstairs Downstairs* and *In Loving Memory*

BECKETT, Thomas-a .... Archbishop of Canterbury.

BELLANEY, Archie .... Conservationist — moved to Canada to be a real Indian. Helped save the Beaver. The subject of Richard Attenborough's new film.

BERKELEY, Ballard .... Actor — played the senile Major in *Fawlty Towers*. Also played Hester's father in *Fresh Fields* and starred in over 100 films, the last of which, prior to his death was National Lampoon's *European Vacation*.

BLACKWELL, Elizabeth .... Doctor — the first female to qualify as a doctor.

BRAND, Jo .... Comedienne.

BREEZE, Hector .... Artist — draws cartoons for the Guardian and Express.

BURTON, James .... Builder — the man who built St. Leonards-on-sea.

CAPEL, Edward .... Playwright and play censor.

CHOP BACKERS, The .... A vicious band of smugglers.

CHURCHILL, Mary .... Daughter of Winston.

COOKSON, Catherine .... Authoress — married at St. Mary Star of the sea.

COWDREY, Chris .... Cricketer.

COWDREY, Colin .... Cricketer.

CROWLEY, Aleister................. Poet, black magician, rapist, murderer and child molester.

DE SAVERY, Peter .... Multi-millionaire businessman and annual entrant for the America's Cup.

ESTELLE, Don....................... Actor — starred in *It Ain't 'alf Hot Mum*.

FURNISS, Harry .... Cartoonist, magazine owner, author, film maker and cinema owner.

GARDNER, Mark .... Lottery millionaire.

GREER, Germaine.................. Author and Women's Lib. campaigner.

HAGGARD, Sir Henry Rider ..... Author — wrote *She* and *King Soloman's Mines* in St. Leonards-on-sea.

HONEYSETT .... Cartoonist.

HOWELL, Derek .... Lord Tiverton — nightclub owner and local parliamentary candidate for the Monster Raving Loony party.

HUNT, James .... Racing driver.

HUNT, Leigh .... Poet.

LEAH, Edward .... Poet.

LIND, Jenny........................ Singer — nicknamed the Swedish Nightingale.

LING, Peter......................... Writer — devised the ATV/Central soap opera *Crossroads*.

LOGIE-BAIRD, John .... Inventor — produced the world's first television picture and radar signal in Hastings.

LOWE, Arthur...................... Actor — starred in *Dad's Army*.

MacDONALD, George............. Writer.

McPHERSON, Graham (Suggs).. Lead singer of the former Ska rock band Madness.

MARTIN, Michael.................. Cartoonist — draws Fred Bassett in the Mail.

MARTINEAU, R. B. .... Artist.

MOGRIDGE, George .... (Old Humphrey) — Writer.

MOORE, Sir John .... General.

NAPOLEON, Louis ....

OATES, Titus....................... Involved in the Popeist Plot.

PATMORE, Coventry .... Poet.

PAYNE, Cynthia.................... Luncheon Voucher Madame.

Prince RANIER of Monaco....... Went to a Hastings boarding school.

ROSSETTI, Dante Gabriel........ Artist — married Elizabeth Siddall at St. Clements Church.

ROUSE, James...................... Artist.

SHAW, Gerald .... Cinema organist.

SIDDALL, Elizabeth .... Poet — married Dante Gabriel Rossetti in Hastings. Committed suicide in the Old Town. Buried at St. Clements Church.

STEVENS, Cat...................... Singer.

STONHAM, Biddy .... Biddy the Tub Man.

SUTCH, David...................... Screaming Lord Sutch — founder member of the Monster Raving Loony Party. 1960s singer and pirate pop ship owner.

WATERHOUSE, Keith............. Cartoonist — drew Flook for the *Mail* and *Mirror* under the name Trog.

WELLESLEY, Arthur .... Duke of Wellington.

WHISTLER, Webster .... Artist.

WILCOX, Toyah.................... Singer and TV Presenter.